# THE MIAMI DOLPHINS

BY JOANNE MATTERN

EPIC

BELLWETHER MEDIA ★ MINNEAPOLIS, MN

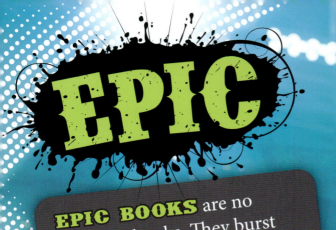

**EPIC BOOKS** are no ordinary books. They burst with intense action, high-speed heroics, and shadows of the unknown. Are you ready for an Epic adventure?

This book is intended for educational use. Organization and franchise logos are trademarks of the National Football League (NFL). This is not an official book of the NFL. It is not approved by or connected with the NFL.

This edition first published in 2024 by Bellwether Media, Inc.

No part of this publication may be reproduced in whole or in part without written permission of the publisher. For information regarding permission, write to Bellwether Media, Inc., Attention: Permissions Department, 6012 Blue Circle Drive, Minnetonka, MN 55343.

Library of Congress Cataloging-in-Publication Data

Names: Mattern, Joanne, 1963- author.
Title: The Miami Dolphins / by Joanne Mattern.
Description: Minneapolis, MN : Bellwether Media, 2024. | Series: Epic. NFL team profiles | Includes bibliographical references and index. | Audience: Ages 7-12 | Audience: Grades 2-3 | Summary: "Engaging images accompany information about the Miami Dolphins. The combination of high-interest subject matter and light text is intended for students in grades 2 through 7"-- Provided by publisher.
Identifiers: LCCN 2023021964 (print) | LCCN 2023021965 (ebook) | ISBN 9798886874853 (library binding) | ISBN 9798886876734 (ebook)
Subjects: LCSH: Miami Dolphins (Football team)--History--Juvenile literature.
Classification: LCC GV956.M47 M28 2024  (print) | LCC GV956.M47  (ebook) | DDC 796.332/640975938--dc23/eng/202305-15
LC record available at https://lccn.loc.gov/2023021964
LC ebook record available at https://lccn.loc.gov/2023021965

Text copyright © 2024 by Bellwether Media, Inc. EPIC and associated logos are trademarks and/or registered trademarks of Bellwether Media, Inc.

Editor: Betsy Rathburn     Designer: Jeffrey Kollock

Printed in the United States of America, North Mankato, MN.

# TABLE OF CONTENTS

| | |
|---|---|
| A SEASON TO REMEMBER | 4 |
| THE HISTORY OF THE DOLPHINS | 6 |
| THE DOLPHINS TODAY | 14 |
| GAME DAY! | 16 |
| MIAMI DOLPHINS FACTS | 20 |
| GLOSSARY | 22 |
| TO LEARN MORE | 23 |
| INDEX | 24 |

# A SEASON TO REMEMBER

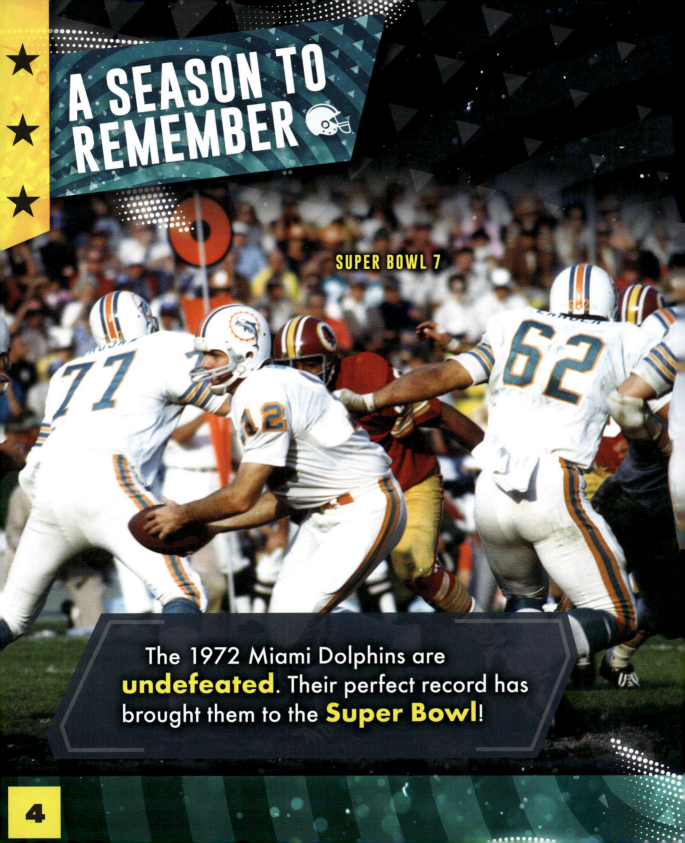

SUPER BOWL 7

The 1972 Miami Dolphins are **undefeated**. Their perfect record has brought them to the **Super Bowl**!

They take an early lead over Washington. Washington scores a **touchdown** late in the game. But it is not enough. The Dolphins complete their perfect season!

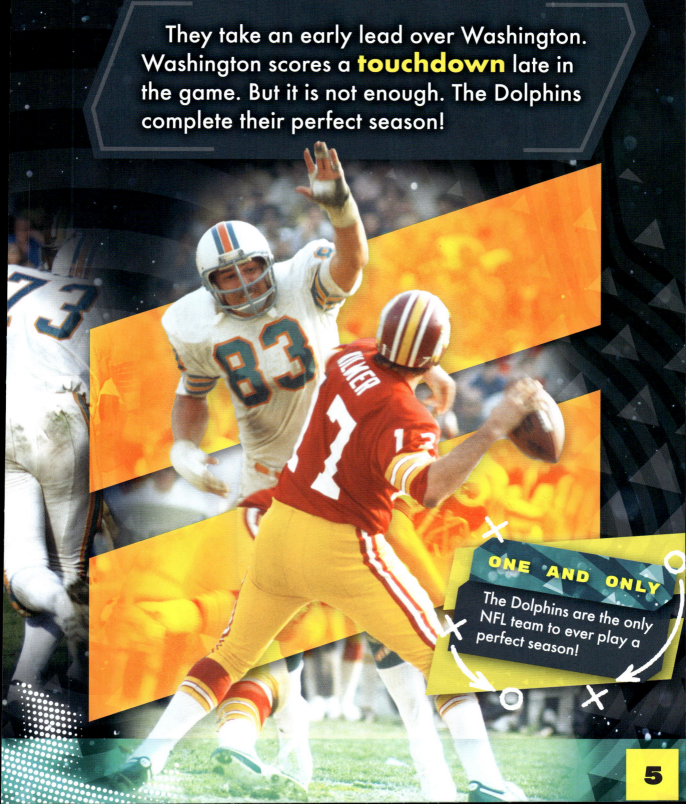

### ONE AND ONLY
The Dolphins are the only NFL team to ever play a perfect season!

# THE HISTORY OF THE DOLPHINS

The Miami Dolphins played their first season in 1966. In 1970, they joined the National Football League (NFL).

That year, Don Shula started as coach. The team added many strong players. They won two Super Bowls in the 1970s!

**TOP COACH!**
When Don Shula retired in 1995, he had won more games than any other NFL coach!

DON SHULA

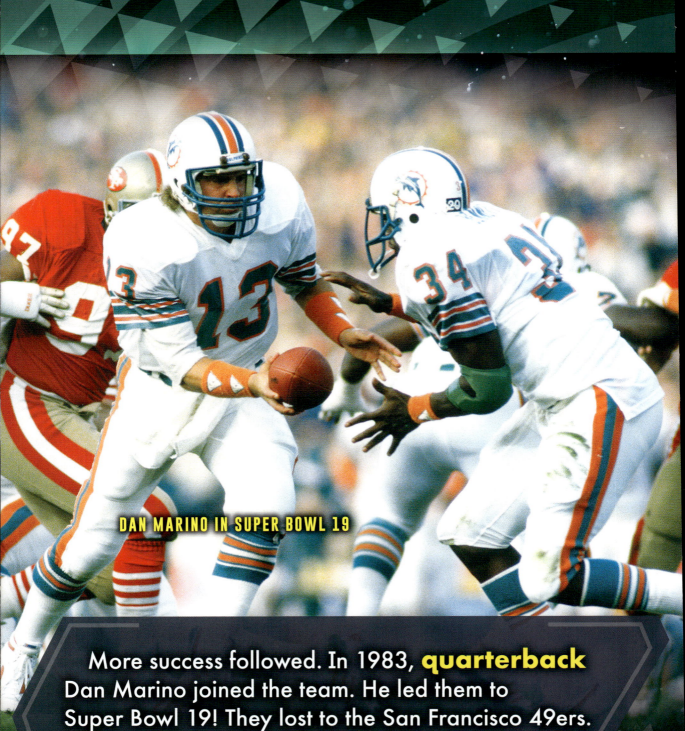

DAN MARINO IN SUPER BOWL 19

More success followed. In 1983, **quarterback** Dan Marino joined the team. He led them to Super Bowl 19! They lost to the San Francisco 49ers.

1995 DOLPHINS GAME

Marino continued to lead the team through the 1990s. He broke many passing records!

Marino left the team after the 1999 season. The Dolphins struggled after he left.

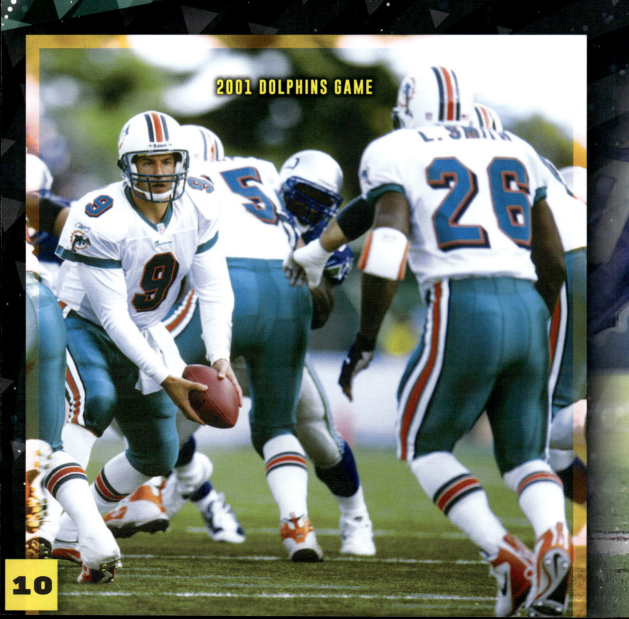

2001 DOLPHINS GAME

The team only made the **playoffs** five times in the 2000s and 2010s. Their only playoff win came in 2000.

2000 PLAYOFF GAME

Still, the Dolphins continued to play hard. In 2022, team leaders such as quarterback Tua Tagovailoa helped the team make the playoffs.

TUA TAGOVAILOA

The Dolphins hope to stay strong and become **champions** again!

## 🏆 TROPHY CASE 🏆

**PLAYOFF** appearances
**24**

**AFC** championships
**5**

**SUPER BOWL** championships
**2**

**AFC EAST** championships
**14**

# THE DOLPHINS TODAY

DOLPHINS VS. JETS

The Dolphins play in the AFC East **division**. They play at Hard Rock **Stadium** in Miami Gardens, Florida.

The Buffalo Bills and the New York Jets are the Dolphins' top **rivals**.

## LOCATION

**HARD ROCK STADIUM**
Miami Gardens, Florida

FLORIDA

# GAME DAY!

Dolphins fans love to support their team! They wear aqua and orange, the team's main colors, to games.

They do a special cheer. They wave their hands on their foreheads. It looks like a dolphin's fin!

The team's **mascot**, T.D., helps fans cheer for their team.

When the Dolphins score a touchdown, the team's fight song plays. Fans love to sing along and cheer for their favorite team!

### THE REAL DEAL

In the 1960s, the team had a live dolphin mascot. The dolphin was named Flipper.

18

## ★ FAMOUS PLAYERS ★

**12 — BOB GRIESE**
Quarterback
Played 1967–1980

**39 — LARRY CSONKA**
Fullback
Played 1968–1974, 1979

**13 — DAN MARINO**
Quarterback
Played 1983–1999

**99 — JASON TAYLOR**
Defensive End
Played 1997–2007, 2009, 2011

**91 — CAMERON WAKE**
Defensive End
Played 2009–2018

# MIAMI DOLPHINS FACTS

LOGO

**JOINED THE NFL** | 1970 (AFL 1966–1969)

**NICKNAME** | The Fins

MASCOT — T.D.

**CONFERENCE** | American Football Conference (AFC)

**COLORS**

**DIVISION** | AFC East

 Buffalo Bills
 New England Patriots
 New York Jets

**STADIUM**

★ HARD ROCK STADIUM ★
opened August 16, 1987

holds 65,326 people

20

# ⏱ TIMELINE

**1966** — The Miami Dolphins play their first season

**1970** — The Dolphins join the NFL

**1973** — The Dolphins win the Super Bowl and finish the season with a perfect record

**1983** — Dan Marino joins the team

**2008** — The Dolphins win the AFC East

# ★ RECORDS ★

**All-Time Passing Leader**
Dan Marino
61,361 yards

**All-Time Rushing Leader**
Larry Csonka
6,737 yards

**All-Time Receiving Leader**
Mark Duper
8,869 yards

**All-Time Scoring Leader**
Olindo Mare
1,048 points

# GLOSSARY

**champions**—winners of a contest that decides the best team or person

**division**—a group of NFL teams from the same area that often play against each other; there are eight divisions in the NFL.

**mascot**—an animal or symbol that represents a sports team

**playoffs**—games played after the regular season is over; playoff games determine which teams play in the championship game.

**quarterback**—a player whose main job is to throw and hand off the ball

**rivals**—long-standing opponents

**stadium**—an arena where sports are played

**Super Bowl**—the annual championship game of the NFL

**touchdown**—a score that occurs when a team crosses into their opponent's end zone with the football; a touchdown is worth six points.

**undefeated**—having never been beaten

# TO LEARN MORE

## AT THE LIBRARY

Hunter, Tony. *Miami Dolphins*. Minneapolis, Minn.: Abdo Publishing, 2020.

Storm, Marysa. *Highlights of the Miami Dolphins*. Mankato, Minn.: Black Rabbit Books, 2019.

Whiting, Jim. *The Story of the Miami Dolphins*. Mankato, Minn.: Creative Education, 2020.

## ON THE WEB

### FACTSURFER

Factsurfer.com gives you a safe, fun way to find more information.

1. Go to www.factsurfer.com.

2. Enter "Miami Dolphins" into the search box and click 🔍.

3. Select your book cover to see a list of related content.

# INDEX

AFC East, 14, 20
cheer, 16, 18
colors, 16, 20
famous players, 19
fans, 16, 18
fight song, 18
Hard Rock Stadium, 14, 15, 17, 20
history, 4, 5, 6, 7, 8, 9, 10, 11, 12, 18
Marino, Dan, 8, 9, 10
mascot, 18, 20
Miami Dolphins facts, 20–21
Miami Gardens, Florida, 14, 15

National Football League (NFL), 5, 6, 20
playoffs, 11, 12
positions, 8, 12
records, 9, 21
rivals, 15
Shula, Don, 6
Super Bowl, 4, 5, 6, 7, 8
Tagovailoa, Tua, 12
timeline, 21
trophy case, 13
undefeated, 4, 5

The images in this book are reproduced through the courtesy of: BOWLL/ AP Images, cover (hero); Timothy T Ludwig/ Getty, p. 3; Focus On Sport/ Getty, pp. 4-5, 5, 7, 8, 19 (Larry Csonka), 21 (1970, 1973, Larry Csonka); Al Messerschmidt Archive/ AP Images, p. 6; Paul Spinelli/ AP Images, p. 9; Tami Tomsic/ Getty, p. 10; ROBERTO SCHMIDT/ Getty, pp. 10-11; Kevin Sabitus/ Getty, pp. 12, 14; Felix Mizioznikov, p. 15; Doug Murray/ AP Images, pp. 16, 16-17; ZUMA Press, Inc./ Alamy, pp. 18-19; George Gojkovich/ Getty, pp. 19 (Bob Griese), 21 (1983, Mark Duper); Icon Sportswire/ Getty, pp. 19 (Dan Marino), 20 (mascot); REUTERS/ Alamy, p. 19 (Jason Taylor); Tribune Content Agency LLC/ Alamy, p. 19 (Cameron Wake); NFL/ Wikipedia, p. 20; Paparazzi, p. 20 (stadium); UPI/ Alamy, p. 21 (2008); Michael Bush/ Alamy, p. 21 (Dan Marino); Tim Umphery/ Getty, p. 21 (Olindo Mare); Cal Sport Media/ Alamy, p. 23.